Master Assignment
Representing Christ on the Job

Charles C. Lake

Evangel Publishing House
Nappanee, Indiana 46550

For information, write to Evangel Publishing House, 2000 Evangel Way, P.O. Box 189, Nappanee, IN   46550.

Toll-Free Order Line: (800) 253-9315
Internet Website:

Cover design by Ted Ferguson, TF Design and Illustration

Publishers Cataloging-in-Publication
(Provided by Quality Books, Inc.)

Lake, Charles C.
     Master assignment: representing Christ on the job /
Charles C. Lake.
     p. cm.
     LCCN 2004104688
     ISBN 1-928915-58-2

     1. Evangelistic work. 2. Witness bearing
(Christianity) 3. Work-Religious aspects
Christianity. I. Title.

               BV3793.L35 2004   269'.2
               QBI33-2018

Printed in the United States of America
10 9 8 7 6 5 4 3 2 1

Dedicated to the memory of
Charles L. Trotter
1919-2000

*whose life in the workplace was the
incarnation of Christian integrity and
left an indelible impression on
my life and ministry.*

Contents

Preface

Professing to be a Christian is easy. Living it out every day is difficult. Being a credible witness for Christ is a constant challenge. Christians live constantly under the scrutiny of unbelievers and nowhere is that more true than in the workplace.

A survey taken recently in the congregation of a large evangelical church found that the one topic more people wished the pastor would address than any other was that of being a witness in the workplace. No Christian can take their faith seriously and not develop a loving concern and a compelling passion for those they relate to daily in their places of employment.

Employees develop invaluable relationships in the workplace. The desire to see a fellow worker share eternity in heaven is the natural outcome in a believer's heart. A sense of indebtedness to an employer who provides the means of a daily livelihood sparks a genuine desire to share life's most valued possession.

If the Great Commission of Christ to His church can be broken down into geographic categories of Jerusalem, Judea, Samaria and the uttermost parts of the earth, the Jerusalem category could be broken down into subcategories such as in the home, in the workplace, in the neighborhood and in society in general. Where in the life of a believer is there a better field to sow the seed of Christian truth and desire a harvest than in one's place of employment? Where is one's witness more needed?

In the 21st. century there are limitations as to how overt a Christian's witness can be but a living witness has great power to open doors of opportunity to respond to inquiring minds who want to know of Christ. The verbal witness may have to take place elsewhere while the right to be heard is won in the daily routine of accomplishing the business for which one is being paid.

If it is true that no one knows better what kind of a Christian you are than those who live under the same roof, it is also true that co-workers in the workplace follow as a close second. An average of forty hours per week spent with the same person or persons in an uncontrolled environment provides ample opportunity for an unbeliever to witness whether or not the principles of professed Christianity really work.

Witnessing in the workplace begins with a basic assumption. The most difficult task in preparing for witness at work is done in the area of one's attitude. What your attitude is about your employer or your employees is foundational. Your attitude toward your fellow employees lays the sub-floor while your work itself provides the framing of your witness. Your attitude about conflict in the workplace builds the roof that protects a positive witness for Christ.

What tools are available to help us acquire and maintain those proper attitudes? There is never a greater source than the Word of God. The Bible has much to say about the relationships of the workplace as well as the attitudes that should drive them.

As we explore these areas of attitude my prayer is that these thoughts will be meaningful and helpful as you look at portions of God's Word, make practical application and daily seek to live out the Word in one of the ripest harvest fields of your world.

1

Christians in Today's Workplace

You are God's children whom he loves, so try to be like him. Live a life of love just as Christ loved us and gave himself for us as a sweet-smelling offering and sacrifice to God (Eph. 5:1–2, New Century Version).

Can you imagine being fined $5,000 for wearing a baseball-style cap to work? Jon Kitna, Cincinnati Bengals quarterback, can. Early in 2004, the National Football League (NFL) enacted such a fine against him.

Apparently, Kitna had violated an NFL rule prohibiting the wearing of non-NFL apparel immediately after a game. Television footage of the quarterback showed him wearing a red cap marked with a white cross as he left the stadium. His attempt to share a silent Christian witness ran afoul of the league's management.

"That's what happens when you don't follow the rules," Kitna was reported as saying. "I won't wear it anymore. The Bible says to submit to the authorities placed above you."

What an extraordinary attitude! In fact, his submissive attitude was ultimately more of a witness than his cap with the cross on it. In the following weeks, Kitna's supporters turned up at games en masse, wearing similar caps. Subsequently, the NFL withdrew the fine. Not everyone has had such favorable results. The Ninth U.S. Circuit Court of Appeals recently ruled that a large computer company was right in firing a worker after he posted Scripture verses in his cubicle. He intended the verses to counter the company's pro-homosexuality diversity campaign posters. The employee was fired when managers determined that the Scripture readings could be viewed as offensive. The court agreed, calling the Scripture verses "demeaning and degrading" for homosexuals.

An "Employee of the Year" in an Indianapolis shipping and warehouse firm found herself in trouble over her habit of saying to others at work, "Have a blessed day." After being ordered to stop, she lodged a discrimination charge with the Equal Employment Opportunities Commission, desiring to protect her religious freedom.

"You never know when the Lord is going to call on you to be His servant, to be a tool, to be a vessel," she said. "I'm just trying to stay focused on the original situation. I want to be able to say, "Have a blessed day," without the threat of being fired."

Some Christians believe that sharing one's faith at work should be more subtle. They would rather witness by example. They shy away from any "in-your-face" type of witness, preferring to do a good day's work and to allow the boss to set the tone of the office.

Others, however, believe that a person's place of employment is the best venue for openly sharing the truth of the gospel. They believe that if they do not aggressively seize the chance, they will forfeit a golden opportunity for witness. All Christians are confronted with the Great Commission to be ambassadors for Christ (Matt. 28:16–20); but what does that mean in the workplace? Our answer will greatly affect our attitude toward our everyday Christian faith and witness.

A pilot who had recently returned from a week-long mission trip to Costa Rica created a small stir in the airline industry in late 2003. It seems the pilot suggested on the plane's intercom that Christians on his flight identify themselves, so that non-Christians could discuss the faith with them.

An airline spokesman said the incident involved "a personal level of sharing that may not be appropriate for one of our employees to do while on the job." A passenger later told a news reporter that the pilot's comments "felt like a threat." She said she and several others aboard were so worried that they tried to call relatives on their cell phones before flight attendants assured them they were safe. Passengers on this flight from Los Angeles to New York's John F. Kennedy Airport will no doubt long remember the incident for a long time.

In 2002, an employee at a General Motors plant in Indianapolis was denied the opportunity to publish in the factory's daily newsletter an invitation for other employees to join him in a lunchtime prayer session on the National Day of Prayer. Knowing that since 1999 the Big Three automaker had permitted employees who share interests to form what it calls "affinity groups," the employee (John Moranski) formally made application for the company to recognize a Christian Employee Network as a GM affinity group. (Such groups are guaranteed the use of the company's facilities for meetings and social events, the use of official communication channels, and the ability to collectively advance their agenda within the company.) The mission statement of Moranski's Christian network was most interesting:

> *The GM Christian Employee Network is a group of GM employees who share a common social identity by having faith in Jesus Christ as Lord and Savior. We exist to provide mutual support, promote strategies for professional development, and to enhance fulfillment of GM Core Values and Business Objectives. We are an interdenominational group and will not promote a particular church or religious denomination in the work-place. We strive to be impartial, sincere, considerate, submissive, non-judgmental, inclusive and full of mercy.*

The statement in no way sought to advocate or promote a particular religious position. The group's four basic objectives were "mutual support, individual respect and responsibility, integrity and teamwork, and customer enthusiasm and increasing market share." What company would object to those?

Yet their application was denied! The company refused to sanction groups that have a "religious or political agenda."

John appealed the company's decision by filing a complaint with the United States Equal Employment Opportunity Commission, on the grounds that GM's ruling violated Title VII of the 1964 Civil Rights Act. (Title VII mandates that companies cannot deny rights and privileges of employment based on religious beliefs.) The EEOC, however, determined that the company's denial of the application did not violate this statute.

At the writing of this book, John Moranski is still pursuing his cause. Most impressive is his Christlike attitude. In no way is he vindictive. His goal is not self-seeking. He is simply taking his stand for individuals to practice their faith in the workplace.

Several para-church organizations have emerged in the evangelical community seeking to penetrate the business world with the gospel of Christ. Some place chaplains in major businesses, while others conduct workshops and seminars to equip believers to be effective witnesses where they work. A brochure advertising one such workshop listed its objective as teaching laymen "how to win the high ground at work in a way that blends a gracious spirit, a keen intellect, a courageous heart, and a cultural sensitivity."   That's a big, but worthwhile order.

In King David's time, soldiers armed for battle were needed to accomplish the purposes of God. Among those who volunteered were the men of Issachar. The Bible says they "understood the times and knew what Israel should do" (1 Chron. 12.:32). Christ still needs men and women who understand the times in which we live and who know how to accomplish the purposes of God in reaching a world.

Each place of employment will differ. The degree of freedom to witness for Christ will vary. A gracious spirit, a keen intellect, a courageous heart, and a cultural sensitivity will be great assets to a believer in effectively representing Christ in the workplace. One's attitude is often more powerful than one's word. So that's what this book is all about—attitude. "Your attitude should be the same as that of Christ Jesus" (Phil. 2:5). Now that's a Master assignment!

2

●

My Attitude Toward
My Employer

[Slaves] should yield to their own masters at all times, trying to please them and not arguing with them. They should not steal from them but should show their masters they can be fully trusted so that in everything they do they will make the teaching of God our Savior attractive (Tit. 2:9–10, New Century Version).

It's relatively easy to profess to be a Christian. It's a challenge, however, to daily live a Christian lifestyle, especially in the workplace.

At home we are around people we know and love, family who tend to be more understanding of our weaknesses and shortcomings. In the neighborhood there is generally less stress, and we often go days or seasons without even seeing those who live next door.

The workplace is different. Five days a week, at least forty hours a week, under the demands and expectations of our employer, we interact with individuals we did not ourselves choose to be our co-workers. Add a profession of knowing Christ, and we find ourselves living in the proverbial fishbowl, with our fellow employees watching our every move to see if indeed we are authentic.

In the early church, most members of the congregation were either slave owners or slaves. So in the Bible we do not read about employers and employees. We read about masters and slaves. It is from those relationships we take the principles that guide us in today's workplace. As we read God's Word, we can supply the words *employer* for *master* and *employee* for *servant* or *slave* to get the relevant teaching of God's Word that is applicable to our daily lives. For example:

> *Teach* employees *to be subject to their* employers *in everything. To try to please them, not to talk back to them, and not to steal from them, but to show that they can be fully trusted, so that in every way they will make the teaching about God our Savior attractive (paraphrase of Tit. 2:9).*

"That the teaching about God our Savior be made attractive"—that is a worthy goal for our performance in the workplace. Before we examine that objective, let me state a personal conviction that shapes the rest of this book: *I believe that most of the work of being effective Christian witnesses in the workplace revolves around our attitudes.* Our attitudes toward our employers, toward our fellow employees, toward our work itself, and toward conflict in the workplace all play an important role in our being positive, effective witnesses for Christ on the job.

To "make the teaching about God our Savior attractive," let's consider four principles found in God's Word that apply to our relationships with our employers. Then we'll see if there's a model employee tucked away somewhere in the Scriptures.

The first principle is found in Proverbs 25:13. : "Like the coolness of snow at the harvest time is a trustworthy messenger to those who send him. He refreshes the spirit of his [employer]." " In other words, *an employee should be faithful and trustworthy.* Can your employer trust you with his possessions? Can he or she trust you to speak the truth, not slanted in your favor to make you look good?

The ability to stand in the workplace as a respected, trustworthy, faithful employee builds an atmosphere in which people listen when you speak of your faith. When you have credibility as a person, your message has credibility. If you're not credible, why should anyone ever believe that your message is true? Faithfulness is a characteristic of every godly employee.

Notice how this principle appears throughout the Old Testament. Consider first Joseph. Joseph was a servant in Potiphar's house, a believer in an ungodly environment. Because Joseph was so faithful, Potiphar trusted into his care everything that he owned, believing that he would manage it well. I suspect that Potiphar was not the most ethical, godly individual to be working for. Yet in the midst of that environment, Joseph proved himself faithful (Gen. 39:1–6).

Nehemiah was a cupbearer to a pagan king (Neh. 1:11). One day he came to work, and his countenance was troubled. The king said to him, "I'm concerned. You're not happy. Why?" "Because my people, the Jews, are exiled, and the city gates of Jerusalem are torn down," Nehemiah replied.

Because of the faithfulness of his employee, this pagan king became so concerned that he not only let Nehemiah off work to go visit the city of Jerusalem and scout out the needs of rebuilding the wall, but he gave him the resources to make it happen (Neh. 2:1–8).

Look at the book of Daniel, where the same thing occurs. Daniel, also living in a pagan environment, proved himself faithful and gained the trust of his employer (Dan. 2).

No matter the environment, no matter what excuse we might conjure up, if we remain faithful in our workplace, we begin to create an atmosphere in which we can speak of our faith with such confidence that others will listen and believe.

2   The Bible's second principle for our attitude toward our employers is found in Colossians 3:22, where we are told that *employees are to be obedient:*

> Servants, obey your earthly employers in everything; and do it, not only when their eye is on you and to win their favor, but with sincerity of heart and reverence for the Lord."

Let's carefully examine that verse. It says we're to obey our employers in everything, unless our obeying would cause us to violate our moral or ethical convictions. I could name any number of believers who have lost their jobs because they have refused to do something their employer asked because they believed it to be unethical. I stand in awe of those individuals who could lovingly say to their employers, "I will not fudge on those figures; I will not lie on that report to make it look better than what it really is. If I did that, I would sin, and I must be accountable to God. If it costs me my job, I will not do what's wrong." Perhaps you resonate with that statement because you once lost your job as a result of refusing to obey an unethical order. That's what you should have done.

A woman once sent me the following letter, requesting my opinion on her final question:

> For eight years I worked for an insurance company that marketed to educators. I was fortunate to work with many Christians and to have many Christian clients. But when my neighbor (and client) filed a claim for hail damage to

his roof, I was faced with an "honesty in the workplace" issue. There was no hail damage to his roof or any others in our subdivision. He was preparing to sell his home and the roof needed to be replaced. Filing an insurance claim was his way of paying for new shingles.

I called the claims department and told them the claim should be denied. They replied that they knew the client had lied, but because he was the superintendent, they would pay the claim. I continued to talk with various people in authority about our responsibility to be honest about the claim, but the moral and ethical issue never seemed important enough to risk alienating an "important" person. After exhausting all of my avenues of appeal, I was told to let it drop. As a Christian did I do enough?

Unlike this woman, however, perhaps our employers' orders do not involve a violation of our moral and ethical convictions; it simply may be a matter of contradicting our personal preference. In that instance, the Bible binds us to obedience. Through obedience to our employers, we earn a credibility that allows us to speak and to be heard.

The third principle is found in the next verse, Colossians 3:23: "Whatever you do, work at it with all your heart, as working for the Lord, and not for men." In other words, *Christian employees work for the Lord*. Whom do you work for? Well, if God's Word is true, we all work for the same Employer. It's with that attitude that we are to go to work each day.

The Bible communicates a high work ethic. "If a man will not work, he shall not eat" (2 Thess. 3:10). By the sweat of our brow we earn our livelihood, the Bible tells us (Gen. 3:19). Yet many employers will tell you that, although some people work so hard that they have to ask them to slow down, others are just lazy. What happens when someone's lazy? It generally means that someone else has to

1 FAITHFUL
2 ETHICAL
3 WORK f th LORD
4 RESPECT

pick up the slack. When that happens and your boss doesn't believe that you are worth your wages, how would you ever share your faith in Jesus Christ with your fellow employees or your employer? We owe our employers our best efforts, giving them a full day's work for a full day's pay.

4. The fourth principle is that *employees should respect their employers.* Read 1 Timothy 6:1–2: "All who are under the yoke of [employment] should consider their [employers] worthy of full respect, so that God's name and our teaching may not be slandered." Note that little phrase, "that our teaching may not be slandered." Look once again at Titus 2:9 and catch the last phrase, "that the teaching about God our Savior might be attractive." We're not to talk back to our employers and not to steal from them. Instead, we are to show them that we can be fully trusted.

When I was a young boy growing up in Kentucky, my dad worked at a steel mill. Dad was a member of the union, and once a year the union asked him to be their representative to go with management to inspect the lockers of the employees. Unannounced inspection of lockers was clearly stated in the company's policy manual; employees knew that it was going to happen. Periodically, a representative of the union and a representative of management would open all the lockers with a pass key to look for stolen company property.

Every inspection day, my dad would come home depressed. I remember asking, "Dad, what's wrong? Why do you feel so bad about your job?" Dad would reply, "Charles, our company's not perfect, but their benefits are more than fair. They treat us employees with respect. They're there for us when we need them. But, Charles, you wouldn't believe the things we get out of lockers." Tools, supplies, and other items owned by the company were stashed away in the employees' lockers. Day by day, slowly and unseen, these things were being stolen. It was always with the attitude: *The company owes me this. They don't pay me enough. This thing is worn out anyway. They're probably getting ready to replace it.* Rationalization and excuses abounded. In reality, these employees were thieves. Obviously, thievery negates a Christian's ability to witness. Try sharing your faith with a co-worker or with your boss when you are perceived as a thief.

Genesis 41:39–40 picks up the story of Joseph, who had proven to be such a good employee for Potiphar:

> Then Pharaoh said to Joseph, "Since God has made all this known to you, there is no one so discerning and wise as you. You shall be in charge of my palace, and all my people are to submit to your orders. Only with respect to the throne will I be greater than you."

There is a place in our walk with the Lord where our commitment to God makes such a difference that, when we enter the workplace, the people who work around us notice. If they don't notice, we will have difficulty ever telling them about the Lord. Joseph earned credibility by his behavior. He manifested not only the gifts given to him by God, but manifested them with a servant's attitude.

What is your attitude toward your employer? If you act as though your employer owes you something, expect one result. If you labor as if you believe you owe your employer your very best, the outcome will be quite different. You are to respect your employer, whether or not he or she deserves it. Christians love unconditionally, as Christ loved. Your working to make your employer successful, to make him look good, will pay tremendous dividends when you attempt to be a winsome witness for Christ.

During one year of my adult life, I worked as a rehabilitation counselor at a mental institution. I was to be the only Christian on one of the teams. The first priority in Monday morning staff meeting was to discuss our activities of the weekend. The boss delighted in describing his sexual escapades. One of our employees would often tell how he came off a drunken binge on Saturday evening and managed to get sobered up to come to work on Monday morning. It was that kind of environment. The team seldom was interested in hearing what I did on weekends. They weren't interested in church stuff.

There would be days when I would go to work feeling discouraged because I had little or no respect as a believer in an unbelieving world. However, it didn't take me long to discover that when any one of my co-workers had experienced a crisis in their life, they sought me out. When they asked to talk with me where no one else could hear, I could anticipate what was going to happen. They would pour their hearts out. I often wanted to say, "Why are you coming to me? Why don't you go to one of the other team members?" But they didn't want to discuss their problems with just anyone. They wanted someone they thought knew God, somebody who could point the way to some answers.

You will have moments on your job when doors are opened to share things of the spirit. Your employer or co-workers will want to listen. Sometimes they only want a quick fix or an easy way out, but sometimes they are really open to the Word of God. To lead them into a right relationship with Christ is the opportunity you have longed and prayed for so often.

I have a recurring dream. I can see the city in which I live, and it's dark, extremely dark. You can't see your hand before you. As a sense of despair begins to come over me, I begin to see little lights being lit, dispelling the darkness. In my dream, those lights illuminate the faces of people in my congregation. I see some who work downtown, some who work in the suburbs, and others who work at home or attend school. They are igniting their witness, and their light is dispelling the darkness. I stop and ask myself, *Is this just a dream, or could this be reality?*

Jesus said on the Mount of the Beatitudes, "You are the light of the world. A city set on a hill cannot be hidden" (Matt. 5:14). There is a way for us to go into the marketplace, into the working world, and not be obnoxious about our faith. In a winsome, credible, and authentic way, we can be witnesses to Christ, manifesting a Christlike attitude that is convincing. Whether our employers and co-workers accept Christ is God's responsibility, not ours. The real issue is this: When we speak, will our co-workers be willing to listen?

As I said earlier, I believe the effectiveness of our witness in the workplace depends upon our attitudes, so it's time for an attitude check. Prayerfully consider your attitude toward your employer and your fellow employees. If your attitude needs to be changed, ask the Master Craftsman to do it for you. Return to work with an attitude like His. Philippians 2:5–8 describes the attitude that brought Christ into our world:

> Your attitude should be the same as that of Christ Jesus:
> Who, being in very nature God,
>> did not consider equality with God something to be
>> grasped, but made himself nothing,
>> taking the very nature of a servant,
>> being made in human likeness.
> And being found in appearance as a man,
>> he humbled himself
>> and became obedient to death—even death on a cross!

"Take the very nature of a servant" and earn the right to be heard. Remember that most of the impact of your witnessing in the workplace depends upon your attitude.

3

My Attitude Toward My Employees

Masters, . . . be good to your slaves. Do not threaten them. Remember that the One who is your Master and their Master is in heaven, and he treats everyone alike (Eph. 6:9, New Century Version).

In this chapter, we will consider four biblical principles that describe how Christian employers should relate to employees. Then we will look for a model employer in Scripture who illustrates those principles.

The first principle is found in Colossians 4:1, which says that *employers are to pay their employees fairly.*

[Employers], provide your [employees] with what is right and fair, because you know that you also have a Master in heaven.

This passage is very similar to Ephesians 6:9. In each case, Paul not only gives instruction but supplies justification for doing so: "because you know that you also have a master in heaven." What is Paul saying? He's saying that, as a Christian employer, you want to treat your employees fairly because you want God to treat you fairly. How you treat your employees affects the way your Master (God) treats you.

Several years ago, I had the privilege of knowing a man who had the reputation of being one of the most godly men ever to live in his town. There was only one problem: He didn't have the respect of many of his employees, because they did not feel they were paid fairly. There was an interesting explanation, however.

He and his wife lived a very frugal lifestyle, so he assumed that everyone else lived as he did. It didn't take much money for him to live on. He worked hard to make all the money he could, so that he might give to others. His primary interest in giving was to Christian missions. He was one of the most generous, giving men that I have ever known. His low company pay scale, however, impacted his witness for Christ in the community. Disgruntled employees believed their boss was raking in the profits. Not knowing of his generosity, his employees simply felt that he was getting rich at their expense. Thus, his witness to his employees was greatly weakened.

The Bible states clearly that a laborer is worthy of his wages (Luke 10:7).

We find the second biblical principle for employers in Deuteronomy 24:15, where the writer says:

> Pay him his wages each day before sunset, because he is poor and counting on it. Otherwise he may cry to the Lord against you, and you will be guilty of sin.

I don't believe the verse literally means that every employer is to pay each employee daily before the setting of the sun. But whether they are paid weekly, bi-weekly, or bi-monthly, *employees should be paid promptly.* The principle of prompt payment applies to other areas of our finances as well. Whatever we owe to anyone, we ought to pay on time. Why? Because their obligations come due, just as ours do. If we fail to pay promptly, we are likely to start a chain reaction that causes others to suffer. When employers begin to defraud their employees or delay the payment of their wages, the Bible labels that a sin. It is wrong that anyone should work and not be paid promptly.

The third principle is that *employers should give consideration to the grievances of their employees.*

> *If I deny justice to my menservants and maidservants when they have a grievance against me, what will I do when God confronts me? What will I answer when called into account? (Job 31:13–14).*

Believers often share with me that they have no channel for airing grievances where they work. Others say that, if they use the grievance process, they are frowned upon or abused. A few say that their grievances are received, considered, and dealt with. The majority, however, speak of employers' pretending to listen, without changing anything. When that is true of a Christian employer, the employer's witness is minimized. Employees feel that the employer doesn't really care about them or their needs.

My mother had a distinguished career in the workplace before her retirement and eventual home-going. Mother was the epitome of perfectionism to a fault. She frequently was acknowledged for the quality of work she produced.

I have a childhood memory of sitting in her office one day, waiting for her to take me to lunch on her lunch break. A client of her firm entered the office and, being unaware of my presence, made a sexually suggestive remark to her. I was young enough that it frightened me.

I will long remember my mother's cool response: "Excuse me sir, I'm a lady and I expect to be treated that way. If you can't speak to me in a proper manner, you are not welcome here." It so happened that her employer was coming around the corner and overheard the entire conversation. My young heart was put at peace when her boss re-echoed her sentiments to his client.

Employers who do listen to the complaints of their employees often discover that they have wisdom beyond their own. Sometimes the employees' suggestions make more money when implemented. Extra profits not withstanding, it ultimately pays to listen. Employees feel valued when their complaint is of concern to their employer.

Ephesians 6:9 gives us the Bible's fourth principle for employers: *Employers should refrain from using threats.*

[Employers], treat your [employees] in the same way. Do not threaten them, since you know that He who is both their master and yours is in heaven, and there is no favoritism with Him.

A number of years ago, while working for a mission organization, it was my privilege to take teenagers to visit mission fields. What a challenge that was! Once, the day before our departure for a trip to Mexico, I was called into the office of my boss. "I have good news and bad news," he told me. I asked for the bad news first. "Your bus driver is ill and cannot drive tomorrow."

Wow, that was a big problem! With a painful look on his face, he said, "We have scouted around everywhere and haven't been able to find a substitute driver."

My response: "Hurry, tell me the good news."

"Well," he said, "we have found a solution, and you're looking at him."

"You, my boss—our bus driver?"

"Yes, I'd be happy to do it if you approve."

I loved and respected the man and enthusiastically agreed that he should go along as our driver. When the first crisis arose on our trip, I looked to him and asked, "What am I to do?"

His response: "I don't know. I'm just the bus driver." That was the nature of our relationship on the entire trip.

We got back from a wonderful trip, several days passed, and then my boss called me into his office. He said, "Charles, I want to discuss the way you handled the trip. I think you did a really good job with one exception, and I hope I can help you learn something that will be helpful on future trips." I had such love and respect for him that he could have confronted me with anything and I would have listened.

"Charles," he said, "sometimes you try to get what you want out of teenagers by threatening them. You don't need to do that. You have their love and respect. Just ask what you want, and they'll respond. You don't have to stoop to threatening."

To this very day, that experience has made me sensitive to this principle. Threatening is a pattern that is very easy to fall into. Parents can easily assume that they must threaten their children, but threats come across harsh and hard. This is why the Bible instructs an employer to avoid threats.

An employer who desires good relationships with employees should remember these four biblical principles:

❑ *Pay employees fairly.*
❑ *Pay employees on time.*
❑ *When employees are unhappy, listen to them.*
❑ *Avoid using threats.*

Does the Bible give us an example of any employer who treated people in this way? Look at Luke 7:

When Jesus had finished saying all this in the hearing of the people, He entered Capernaum. There a centurion's servant, whom his master valued highly, was sick and about to die. The centurion heard of Jesus and sent some elders of the Jews to Him, asking Him to come and heal his servant. When they came to Jesus, they pleaded earnestly with Him, "This man deserves to have you do this, because he loves our nation and has built our synagogue." So Jesus went with them.

He was not far from the house when the centurion sent friends to say to him: "Lord, don't trouble yourself, for I do not deserve to have you come under my roof. That is why I did not even consider myself worthy to come to you. But say the word, and my servant will be healed. For I myself am a man under authority, with soldiers under me. I tell this one 'Go,' and he goes; and that one, 'Come,' and he comes. I say to my servant, 'Do this,' and he does it."

When Jesus heard this, he was amazed at him, and turning to the crowd following him, he said, "I tell you, I have not found so great faith even in Israel." Then the men who had been sent returned to the house and found the servant well (Luke 7:1–10).

I challenge employers to dissect that passage. Look at this employer who, when an employee became ill, made the illness his concern—so much so that he did whatever was necessary to help him in that situation. Over the years I have observed employees with serious illnesses whose employers essentially mark them off the payroll, wanting to be done with them. I've seen other employers who have bent over backwards to be gracious and merciful to people that were going through a time of trial. What a prime time for witness!

Notice also that the centurion, who was in a position of authority, recognized that he himself was under authority. When you reach the top of the human accountability structure, the next level is always divine. Your superior is God! As someone with employees accountable to you, realize that you are accountable to God. You are to be a witness to them, one who treats them in a way in which God would have His children treated.

If you are an employer, how do you measure up? How accurately do these four principles describe your witness to your employees?

4

●

My Attitude Toward
My Fellow Worker

Be wise in the way you act with people who are not believers, making the most of every opportunity. When you talk, you should always be kind and pleasant so you will be able to answer everyone in the way you should (Col. 4:5–6, New Century Version).

Parents appreciate an elementary school principal who refers to her employees as "members of the team." Another educator uses the analogy of a family: They're just one big family, and the principal is called, "Big Daddy." The workaday world has some creative ways of building teams of workers to accomplish a purpose.

But as Christians, do we see our co-workers differently? What should our attitude be toward those whom we refer to as our "fellow workers"?

I want to suggest that our attitude toward our fellow workers should be shaped by three criteria: (1) how we envision them, (2) how we engage them, and (3) how we influence them.

First, how do we envision our co-workers? As I read through the Gospels, I am always impressed with the number of times that the Bible says Jesus was "moved with compassion" for the people He saw (e.g., Matt. 9:36; 14:14; 20:34). You might find it interesting to note that the New Testament uses the phrase, "moved with compassion," only to refer to Christ and no one else. When you study the word compassion in the original language of the New Testament, you find that it expresses one of the strongest, deepest feelings of a person's heart. So the Bible tells us that Jesus was moved with compassion toward the sick, the hungry, and the lonely. Matthew 9 says Jesus was moved with compassion for those who look like sheep without a shepherd—bewildered, depressed, and downtrodden. Jesus saw people through the eyes of compassion.

I challenge you to join me in an experiment. I have been making it a habit, as I read my daily newspaper or listen to the evening news, to measure how long it takes for me to hear about somebody that I have a negative feeling toward. This week the local newspaper told about a man in our county who killed his infant son out of spite for his wife. He was sentenced to life imprisonment. The grandparents of the infant thought that punishment was far better punishment than executing him, because they wanted him to live out the rest of his life remembering every day the crime that he committed. What do you feel toward the man who murdered his infant son? How do you feel toward the grandparents who delight in the vengeance of seeing him tormented for the rest of his life? How would Jesus see them? Would He not be moved with compassion for a man who allowed the seed of bitterness to develop in his life to the extent that he would kill his own infant son? Would He not be moved with compassion for the grandparents who allowed that same seed of bitterness to bear fruit in their lives, so that they relished this man's punishment for the rest of his life? If we begin to look at people through the eyes of Christ, we begin to perceive them differently.

Last night's news broadcast told of a drunken driver who ran into an older couple on their way to a family celebration on the northeast side of Indianapolis. One spouse was killed, and the other was left alone. The drunken driver had been previously arrested for drunken driving; now he kills. Do you feel compassion for the drunk? Compassion for the spouse who remains to live out his days alone? Or do you feel only anger and bitterness? If we begin to look at people through the eyes of Christ, we begin to perceive them differently.

Now think about your attitudes toward others in the workplace. How do you deal with what appears to be a threat from another employee, or jealousy that begins to swell up within you toward a co-worker? Compassion is the key. If somehow we could see people through God's eyes and not our own!

The young man who killed his infant son and the drunken driver who ended a lifelong marriage are individuals who are loved with God's infinite love. They're people for whom God sent His Son to Calvary to die. How then can I begin to devalue any person in my sphere of influence? How can I sit in judgment to condemn them? As a Christian, how can I do anything other than look at them through the eyes of Christ's compassion and relate to them in love, no matter what they do to me, no matter what threat they may pose to me?

I once heard an evangelist tell about a woman who attended a camp meeting where he had preached on the subject of personal holiness. To impress the preacher, this lady engaged him in conversation after the service. She said, "I just loved your message, and I so much believe in what you just said! . . . The other day we had new neighbors move into our neighborhood, and I just kind of pulled back the curtain and watched them as they unpacked. You wouldn't believe that woman. She was just so scantily dressed it was almost lewd. You could have scraped the cosmetics off her face with a knife, and she had a cigarette hanging out of the corner of her mouth. I heard a couple of words of profanity come out of her mouth. And I want you to know I just determined in my heart that I'm not having anything to do with a woman like her."

She missed the point of compassion, didn't she? Her attitude is not compassion; it's what we call *disengagement*.

That brings us to the Bible's second principle: *How do we engage our co-workers?* Remember that when Jesus prayed for you before He went to the cross, He said, "My prayer is not that you take them out of the world but that you protect them from the evil one" (John 17:15). God wants us to engage ourselves in the lives of people who do not share our faith. He expects us to become involved with them in a meaningful relationship that ultimately will earn for us the right to share our faith with them in a way that is convincing, convicting, and compelling.

There's a parable in the teachings of Jesus that probably has sparked more controversy among Bible interpreters than any other. It's found in Matthew 11, beginning in verse 16. Jesus says:

> "To what can I compare this generation? They are like children sitting in the marketplaces and calling out to others: 'We played the flute for you, and you did not dance; we sang a dirge, and you did not mourn.'"

Does that make any sense to you? It didn't to me the first time I read it, so I delved into several Bible commentaries and began to study it. Then the meaning began to unfold. When you were a child, did you ever play house? Did you ever play wedding? I did. I don't think we ever played funeral. But Jesus speaks of some children who sometimes play wedding and at other times play funeral. They said to other children, "We played our flute to make you joyous, but you wouldn't play wedding with us. We played a dirge that we might mourn, but you didn't want to play funeral, either. So we did nothing. We stopped playing to you." Jesus said that He and John the Baptist received that sort of response. Their hearers found fault with whatever they said. Ultimately, they made no response at all to the gospel.

Jesus said that John came neither eating nor drinking, and they accused him of having a demon. Jesus came eating and drinking, and they called Him a glutton and a drunkard, a friend of tax collectors and sinners. So the gospel was presented in two very different ways by John the Baptist and Jesus, and people rejected them both. Here is one of the best contrasts between confrontational evangelism and lifestyle evangelism, John being one and Jesus being the other.

Some people in our congregation can easily learn the Four Spiritual Laws and the two penetrating questions asked by Evangelism Explosion. They can go into their workaday world and confront people with the claims of Christ. Many times, they can lead people to Christ right on the spot. They do it with such tact and grace that I just marvel. They are evangelists gifted to do the job. That was true of John the Baptist.

The Bible says Jesus' critics called him a glutton, a drunkard, a friend of tax collectors and sinners. I don't mean to sound disrespectful, but Jesus was reputed to be a "party animal." If someone was throwing a party, He went to it.

Jesus' first miracle was performed at a marriage supper in Cana of Galilee. Another time, He saw an ornery tax collector sitting up in a sycamore tree, waiting to see Him, and He said, "Come down. I want to go home with you for dinner." Why did Jesus want to go home with this tax collector? Because He had an agenda. He wanted to build a relationship with this man, so that he could ultimately see himself as God saw him, then see himself as he could be in Christ, a new creation.

My point is simply this. If Jesus, our model, could engage the lost in warm personal relationships—if He ate with them, drank with them, struck up conversations with them—should we not be doing the same? How long has it been since you invited an unbeliever into your home to share fellowship, to build relationship, to earn the right ultimately to share your faith in the person of the Lord Jesus Christ?

In his book, *Lifestyle Evangelism*, Joe Aldridge says that within the first two years of our walk with the Lord, most of us divorce ourselves from all of our unchristian friends and become members of the "Holy Huddle." We love to fellowship with the people of God while sinners go untouched with the gospel.

So I go into the workplace, and I envision my co-workers differently. I see them as people God loves with an infinite love, so much of a love that He sent His Son to die for them. They may have lousy values. They may hold political and theological positions that are repugnant to me. But Christ still loves them. He still died for them. He still has compassion upon them. Why shouldn't I?

In the previous chapter, I mentioned that I worked as a counselor at a mental rehabilitation facility for a year. Vicki and I had a major dilemma when the time came for the hospital's Christmas office party: Should we go or shouldn't we go? I said to Vicki, "We're going." The printed invitation told us what to bring, and at the bottom it said, "B.Y.O.B." (bring your own booze). We took 7-Up and went to the party. Everyone there knew us. We ate together, we relaxed together, we built some relationships. It wasn't long into the evening until some of the participants began to get a bit too much of the booze that they had brought. A couple of the men began making passes at other men's wives, mine included, so I simply stated, "It's been a lovely evening. We've enjoyed being here, but it's time for us to go." Very politely, we excused ourselves and left the party.

Monday morning came. We were sitting in staff meeting in our department, and people began talking about the party. Someone exclaimed, without thinking, "We really had a blast after the preacher left!"

The boss, a very ungodly man, very quietly said, "Yes, and that should tell us something, shouldn't it?" And nothing more was said about the party.

God will not be left without a witness. You don't have to compromise your convictions to penetrate the world, to engage with unbelievers. You can build relationships so that the day may come when the door of opportunity swings open and a co-worker says, "I see something in you that I don't see in everybody else, and I want what you've got."

Third, how do you influence your co-workers? We influence people as we live what I want to call the exceptional Christian life. You're not going to be an effective Christian witness in the workplace if you're just a "good ol' Joe." There are a lot of them in the world. I had co-workers at the hospital who would have done anything for me. They were just simply good, moral people. But they didn't know Jesus. In the light of eternity they will be condemned by their disbelief. So just being good in their presence isn't good enough. Evangelism calls for an exceptional lifestyle.

The Bible says, "Be wise in the way you act toward outsiders; make the most of every opportunity" (Col. 4:5). As we relate with unbelievers in the workplace, we need wisdom. Recently, I stood chatting with one of our newly appointed county officials. In a very loving way, I said to him, "I prayed for your predecessor. I'm going to pray for you, too." This took him back a bit, so I added, "I'm praying for you because you need wisdom that you don't have to do your job."

He stood there for a moment and said, "I guess you're right."

I said, "I know Someone who's got that wisdom, and if you ask Him, He'll give it to you."

He replied, "I want to mull that over."

When you go into the workplace and you're dialoging with people who don't share your faith, you need wisdom you don't have. You get up in the morning and say, "Lord, as I go to my sanctuary, may everyone who comes within the sphere of my influence make contact with the love of God, radiating through me. Lord, give me the wisdom to say the right things and know when to keep my mouth shut." So be wise in the way you act toward outsiders.

Then consider the way you talk. "Let your conversation be always full of grace" (Col. 4:6). Are you a gracious person? Do the words that come out of your mouth bring encouragement and healing to other people, or are they demanding your rights or vengeance? Perhaps someone in your workplace is so irritating that everybody tends to shun that individual. Not you. You tend to be drawn to that person because they're lonely. You want them to have a friend, and you show them grace, not only by the way you act but by the way you speak. Your conversation is always full of grace and "seasoned with salt" (v. 6). What does salt do? Commentators tell us that the people of New Testament times primarily used salt as a preservative. So Paul's readers understood that their "salty" conversation should promote life, wholeness, and health.

"So let your conversation be full of grace, seasoned with salt, so that you may [have the wisdom to] know how to answer everyone" (v. 6). Your unbelieving co-worker may say, "Now that you're speaking of spiritual things, I've always had a question. Maybe you can help me. Where did Cain and Abel get their wives?" God will give you wisdom to say, "I don't know, and I don't suppose that anybody really does. That isn't a terribly relevant question to me. I'm more concerned with. . . ." And you bring the conversation back to what's important.

I traveled to Portland, Oregon, one evening to preach, and the plane was late. I got there in time to be taken directly from the airport to Treemont Evangelical Church. The man who picked me up had waited three hours for my plane to arrive. I asked, "What did you do for those three hours?"

He said, "I was witnessing to somebody about Jesus."

"Did you win him?" I asked.

"No, I got hung up."

"What did you get hung up on?"

My driver sighed. "He wanted to know whether the fire in hell is literal fire or not. For the life of me, I couldn't convince him."

I asked, "Why did you waste your time even trying?" To an unbeliever, that's not a relevant issue. The issue is whether or not a person believes in Jesus. Until a person comes into a right relationship with Christ and has the Holy Spirit within, to enlighten the mind, that person probably could not comprehend that there is a literal fire in hell, let alone know for sure that there is a hell.

First Peter 2:21 gives us another description of exceptional Christian living: "To this you were called, because Christ suffered for you, leaving you an example, that you should follow in his steps." This statement occurs in a paragraph about how slaves ought to submit to their masters—even masters that are unbearable, that accuse them falsely, that cause them to suffer in ways they ought not to ever suffer. Peter says when this happens in the workplace, Christians are not going to follow the natural tendency of the old nature. Instead, they are going to follow the example of Christ. Jesus didn't stand in Pilate's hall and say, "Look here, fellows, I demand my rights." He stood as a lamb before his shearers and he never opened his mouth to defend himself. They called him everything in the book, but he stood there with a smile of radiance on his face, never opening his mouth to defend himself. When they threw the stones and drove the nails into his hands, even when they pierced his brow with a crown of thorns, He never once looked at them and said, "My day's coming; I'll get even with you." He looked at them with compassion, praying that the Father would not lay that sin against their charge. That's exceptional living.

John Wesley, the founder of the Methodist church, came to America to convert the Indians, only to find that he himself was not converted. On the ship back to England, when the storms raged and the Moravian people had a hymn-sing in the middle of the storm, John Wesley said, "Those people have something I've got to have."

Saul of Tarsus breathed out threats against Christians, believing that every time he put a Christian to death he was doing God a favor. He stood and held the cloaks of the men who stoned the evangelist Stephen to death. He heard Stephen say, "Lord, do not hold this sin against them" (Acts 7:60).   And it wasn't long until Saul embraced the faith of that man.

A Roman centurion standing at the foot of the cross heard a dying man pray, "Father, forgive them, for they do not know what they are doing" (Luke 23:34). And the centurion declared, "Surely he was the Son of God!" (Matt. 27:54).

Being good won't cut it. We must come to that place where we die to ourselves, not really caring what people say about us, be it unjust or not. Our chief concern is God's approval, that in all things we walk in obedience to the Lord's command, demonstrating His likeness, believing that He will care for us and in time reveal to our co-workers that the Christian life is not the ordinary, run-of-the-mill type living. It's exceptional because Jesus lives in us. He reigns in us. He does His work through us.

That's a big order. It means that you and I will begin to regard the people with whom we work differently than we ever have before. We will begin to see them as people whom God loves with an everlasting love. We will understand that nothing can separate them from His love. If they kill their infant children, destroy the lives of innocent elderly people, or do any number of other horrible things, God goes on loving them. Nothing they do can diminish His love.

"For God did not send his Son into the world to condemn the world, but to save the world through him" (John 3:17). So we never give up hope that God might redeem the lives of our unbelieving co-workers. Jesus says, "As the Father has sent me, I am sending you" (John 20:21). So we look at our co-workers differently. We never think of ourselves as being better than they. In fact, the Bible says to "consider others better than yourselves" (Phil. 2:3). We want to engage them. We want to build relationships with them. We want to earn the right to be heard with credibility. So when things don't go the way we think they should in the workplace, we don't organize an opposition party. When we're passed over for the job that we think we should have gotten instead, we congratulate the person who got the promotion. We speak with grace and pray that we will have opportunity to speak on behalf of Christ and His people. On Monday morning, if somebody talks about the weekend, we can say, "We had a great weekend, too. We had a great time at our church on Sunday."

Joe Aldridge says, that we Christians have two awesome tools for evangelism: a healthy church and a healthy family. Imagine the impact of being able to say to a co-worker, "I just love my wife. I just love this thing called parenthood. At every stage of parenthood, it gets better and better. It's awesome. You know, it wouldn't have been that way if we hadn't made Christ the center of our home." Don't you think that's going to get people's attention? Marriages are breaking up all around us, but you're out there telling your friends your marriage is wonderful.

Imagine the impact of saying on Monday morning, "It's good to be part of the family of God, where we bear one another's burdens. We all hurt when one of us hurts and rejoice when one rejoices." Unbelievers think that church is boring, lifeless, or contentious. We're out there telling the true story, in hopes that someday one of our acquaintances will say, "I want what you've got. Tell me how to find the way to Jesus."

Whether it's John the Baptist's type of confrontational evangelism or Jesus' type of lifestyle evangelism, we need to share the good news with people who work alongside us. General William Booth, who founded the Salvation Army, once was visiting New York City with his little Salvation Army Band. They were playing their tambourines and singing gospel songs, passing out tracts, and preaching on a street corner. This offended an elegant Christian lady who came walking by. She said, "Excuse me, sir, but your methods of evangelism embarrass me."

General Booth replied, "I'm sorry, ma'am. Pray tell me, what are your methods?"

She thought about that for a moment and said, "Well, I guess I have none."

"Then, ma'am, one thing is for sure," General Booth smiled, "I like my methods better than yours."

What's your method of evangelism? Is it just an ideal? Or can you point to someone in your workplace whose name is written in the Lamb's Book of Life because God used you to reach them?

5

My Attitude Toward My Work

Why spend your money on something that is not real food? Why work for something that doesn't really satisfy you? Listen close-ly to me, and you will eat what is good; your soul will enjoy the rich food that satisfies (Isa. 55:2, New Century Version).

Have you ever noticed how many different words we use in English to denote our work? We can talk about it first of all as a *job*, which connotes a way of making money. The primary purpose of a job is to obtain security. If I have a job, I have a means of paying my bills; if I don't have a job, I lack security in life.

Second, we might refer to our work as our *vocation* or our *profession*. This is a type of work for which someone is especially suited or trained, so it also suggests a sense of identity. You meet someone and naturally ask, "What is your name? Where do you live? What do you do?" Often a person's profession or vocation will trigger certain stereotypes in our mind, which help us identify what kind of person this is.

Third, we may refer to our work as our *career*. A career suggests a sense of achievement or advancement. A career is measured in terms of success. When someone says, "I've had a career in the ministry," or, "I've had a career in sales," the emphasis is upon being successful in that line of work.

What if all of us referred to our work as a *calling*? A calling suggests a commitment to an activity that is fulfilling, in and of itself. A person with a calling says, "I enjoy doing what I do, so I would do it whether or not someone paid me to do it. I'm called to do it." Wouldn't that sense of calling make a difference in our attitudes when we got up in the morning to go about our work?

I've treasured through the years a brief acquaintance with Dr. Gordon McDonald. Every year, I reread his book, *Ordering Your Private World*. He says in that book that we find two kinds of people in the workplace: those who are driven and those who are called. He gives eight characteristics of a person who is driven. Let me list them for you. A driven person is one who:

1. Is most often gratified by accomplishment.
2. Is preoccupied with the symbols of accomplishment.
3. Is caught up in the uncontrolled pursuit of expansion.
4. Tends to have a limited regard for integrity.
5. Often possesses limited or undeveloped people skills.
6. Tends to be highly competitive.
7. Often possesses a volcanic force of anger.
8. Is abnormally busy.

If four or five of these characteristics describe you, it's likely that you are a driven person. By way of contrast, says Gordon McDonald, a called person:

1. Understands that life is a stewardship.
2. Knows exactly who he/she is.
3. Possesses an unwavering sense of purpose.
4. Makes an absolute commitment to that purpose.

Now let me illustrate. In Stuart Briscoe's book, *Extraordinary Living for Ordinary Men*, he tells the story of a small group in his church that meets together for the first time. They were going around the circle, introducing themselves by telling their name, where they lived, and what they do—their occupation. They came to a young woman who told her name and where she lived. When they asked her, "What do you do?" her response was, "I am a disciple of Jesus Christ very skillfully disguised as a machine operator." Nothing could say it better. That young woman had a sense of divine calling.

Let me give you a definition of what I think it means to be called: *A calling means doing what God wants you to do, where God wants you to do it.* If you believe that you go to your place of work to do what God wants you to do, where God wants you to do it, you have a sense of divine call upon your life. You know that you're not working for yourself but for God. You know what God wants you to do each day. As you work with unswerving commitment to the purpose for which God has put you there, your life becomes a witness, even before you open your mouth. Your job is a calling, not simply a job.

Second Corinthians 5:17 says, "Therefore, if anyone is in Christ, he is a new creation; the old has gone, the new has come!" Isn't that wonderful? But don't stop there. The apostle Paul goes on to say in verses 18 and 20:

> All this is from God, who reconciled us to Himself through Christ and gave us the ministry of reconciliation. . . . We are therefore God's ambassadors, as though God were making his appeal through us.

When you understand what the Scripture is teaching here, you realize that the woman in Stuart Briscoe's small group caught a truth that Christians often fail to comprehend. You may be a machine operator; you may be a sales clerk in a department store; you may be an attorney in an office of law; you may be a doctor in a medical office; but you are first and foremost a disciple of Jesus Christ who has been given the ministry of reconciliation. You are in your particular place of work to be a witness of God's redeeming love. If you know that you're doing what God wants you to do, where God wants you to do it, you're just as called of God as the preacher is who stands in the pulpit on Sunday morning to preach the Word.

I read recently a statement by Oswald Chambers that clarifies this point. Chambers said, "It is easier to serve God without a call because you're not bothered by what God requires. Common sense is your guide and you veneer it over with Christian sentiment. But if once you receive a commission from Jesus Christ, the memory of what God wants will always be your life goal and you'll no longer be able to work for Him on a common-sense basis." Powerful, isn't it? So whether you are selling cars at the local Ford dealership, selling lights at The Light Gallery, or treating children in the dental office, you are a disciple of the Lord Jesus, given the message of reconciliation to bring people into peace and harmony with God. The job by which you make your living is only a vehicle, a tool that you use to accomplish the purpose for which God has placed you there. What a difference it would make in the workplace if every one of us had that sense of divine calling!

Gordon McDonald gives us another important insight into the Christian attitude toward work. He says that you and I should consider our venue, the place where we work, as a sanctuary instead of a workplace. McDonald tells how a man came to his office one day and said, "I am very jealous of you as a pastor."

"Why?"

The man said, "Because you're called of God to do what you do. You do it among the best people on earth, believers. And when you go to work on Sunday morning, you do it in a beautiful sanctuary. Me? For eight hours every day I drive a bus. Day after day, week after week, month after month, year after year, I spend my time in a *bus*."

Gordon McDonald thought for a moment and gave him this response: "Every morning when you go to work and get aboard that bus, make this statement: `In the name of Jesus, I declare this bus a sanctuary for the next eight hours. And I declare that all the people

who enter this sanctuary will experience the love of Christ ...
me, whether they realize it or not.'"

That's an awesome idea, isn't it? To think that where you work is
not just a workplace. In God's eyes, it can be a sanctuary. You can
pray that every day when you go into your workaday sanctuary,
everyone who comes within your sphere of influence will experience
the love of God through you, as you assist those individuals in the
way of your calling or make whatever you make with your hands.
You do your work with the love of Christ. What a difference that
attitude would make in the impact of your work!

I have loved for years the Scripture text of Romans 12:1–2. Most
Christians can quote it from memory:

> *I beseech you therefore, brethren, by the mercies of God, that ye
> present your bodies a living sacrifice, holy, acceptable unto God,
> which is your reasonable service (kjv).*

When the Jews of New Testament times went into the temple to
worship, they went to offer dead sacrifices as tributes to the Lord,
and they did it on the Sabbath. But in this text, Paul is saying that
worship isn't just something we do on Sunday morning. It's a seven-
day-a-week, twenty-four-hour-a-day activity for the believer. You
are called to worship the Lord all the days of your life—all the hours
of the day, every minute of the hour—and you do it not by bringing
dead sacrifices, but by presenting your life as a sacrifice of praise and
adoration to the Lord. The New International Version says this is
"your reasonable spiritual act of worship."

So you and I get up in the morning called of God to do what we
are going to do for this day. We are called to be Christ's disciples in
the workplace. In fact, ours is not just a workplace, but a sanctuary
where everyone who comes within our sphere of influence will experience the love of Christ. The place where you and I labor is a sanctuary where we practice our calling.

Third, we also should consider our work to be a towel and basin, not a ladder to be climbed. The gospel of John tells us about that moment in the Upper Room, prior to the breaking of the bread, when Jesus teaches His disciples one of the greatest lessons He'll ever teach them, and He does it without opening His mouth. He just gets up from the table, picks up a towel and a basin, and stoops to wash His disciples' feet (John 13:1–17).

John is the only one of the four Gospels that mentions the washing of the disciples' feet. But Luke says that, while they were together in the Upper Room—probably prior to Jesus' washing their feet—the disciples were arguing about which of them would be greatest in the kingdom that Jesus would establish (Luke 22:24–30). Who would sit on His right hand, and who would sit on His left hand? I believe that in this moment, Jesus began to teach them a lesson they would never forget.

If you have visited the Holy Land, you understand why the disciples' feet needed to be washed after walking the dusty paths of Jerusalem, the Holy City. Not only did their feet get dirty, but they got tired and hot. So in Bible times, it was customary to have a servant greet visitors at the door, take off their sandals, bathe their feet, and cool them from the hot pavement so that the guests could relax and enjoy their visit. But when the disciples came to the Upper Room, there were no servants present. Not one of the Twelve offered to wash the feet of the others. (How could they? They were busy arguing over which one of them was the greatest!) So the disciples sat down to eat with dirty, hot feet. Jesus got up, girded himself with a towel, took a basin, and stooped to wash the feet of the disciples. As He had told the quarreling brothers, James and John, "Whoever wants to become great among you must be your servant, and whoever wants to be first must be slave of all" (Mark 10:43–44).

So we go into the workplace, not looking for a ladder to climb, but for a towel and the basin with which to serve. We remember Joseph, Nehemiah, and Daniel—constantly being promoted, constantly being rewarded by the kings that they served—not because they climbed a ladder of achievement but because they served people through the love of God.

Fourth, we also should consider God to be our Evaluator. Recall that Colossians 3:23–24 says:

"Whatever you do, work at it with all your heart, as working for the Lord, not for men, since you know that you will receive an inheritance from the Lord as a reward. It is the Lord Christ you are serving."

The staff members of our congregation do evaluations of one another each year. I'll evaluate the associate pastor. The associate pastor will evaluate all of the staff pastors. The pastors will evaluate their administrative assistants and the custodians. A committee of three elders will evaluate me, the senior pastor. Finally, each staff member sits down with the evaluators and walks through the report. We will see what others believe we are doing well. We will see the areas where they perceive weakness, and we'll turn those areas of weakness into goals for growth and improvement for the year to come. Such an evaluation can be a very positive experience, and it ought to be a normal part of any workplace.

But I have to remember one thing: I'm not here ultimately to please my three elders. I'm accountable to Someone greater. No matter what they say about how well or how poorly I do my job, someday I'll stand before Almighty God. He will evaluate the work that I have done, and I will be rewarded accordingly.

Christians go into the workplace with that kind of attitude. We put forth our best effort, not for job advancement, not to make more money, but because we do our work as unto the Lord. Believers recognize that ultimately they're accountable to God.

So I leave you with these four questions, and I dare you to answer them honestly before the Lord:

1. Are you a driven person, or a called person?

2. Do you consider your place of work to be just your work station, or is it your sanctuary where you worship the Lord?
3. Are you climbing the ladder of success, or handling the towel and basin of service?
4. Do you work as if you're doing it all for the Lord, before whom someday you will stand and *give an account for your life?*

A Christian witness in the workplace begins by getting our attitudes right. Then the witness inevitably will come.

6

My Attitude Toward Conflict in the Workplace

You yourselves know that you should live as we live. We were not lazy when we were with you. And when we ate another person's food, we always paid for it. We worked very hard night and day so we would not be an expense to any of you (2 Thess. 3:7–8, New Century Version).

Conflict in the workplace is inevitable. When it comes, we have a choice: We become either troublemakers or peacemakers.

We can defuse conflicts with our employers by following the biblical principles we saw in chapter 2. First, we learned that we should obey our employers. Recently, a woman called to tell me that she had been fired from her employment. I sensed she was seeking pity, not a solution, so I said, "Why did you get fired?"

She said, "Because I didn't do what the boss told me to do."

"Why didn't you?" I asked.

"Because I thought I knew a better way to do it," she replied.

53

"When I did it my way, I messed up royally." Then she said, without any word from me, "If only I had done what I was told!"

Unless we are asked to violate our moral or ethical convictions, the Bible says we are to obey those in authority over us in the workplace. We are to obey them with sincerity of heart and with reverence, the same attitudes we show toward the Lord.

Second, the Bible told us to respect our employers. First Timothy 6:1 says we are to count our employers "worthy of full respect." In the original language of the New Testament, the word respect literally means "to give value to something." We ought to be lifting up our employers, affirming them. Titus 2:9 says we are to "be subject to" our employers. Again, the original language uses a very interesting word, a military term that means we are to rank ourselves under our employer. Simply put, we've got to remember who's boss. Sometimes we forget that people become our superiors not simply by patronizing the owner of a business, not through nepotism as part of the owner's family. Many people are put in places of authority and leadership because they have earned the right to be there. Therefore, we owe them our respect and obedience.

I have a letter that someone sent to a former employer more than a year after leaving his employment. Here is an excerpt:

> As you know, I struggled at times in dealing with your method of management. As I look back upon it now I have begun to understand better why you did what you did. The purpose of this letter is just to tell you how much I appreciate you for who you are, for what you are, and to tell you that in the past year I have experienced a time of increased understanding in many areas. I now understand some of the struggles you must have gone through at times. This was difficult for me to see while I was working for you and so close to the situation, but I have begun to understand it now in retrospect. Also, I am confronted with some of the same situations and decisions that you

dealt with. The bottom line is this: I have nothing but respect for you. I also have greater respect and appreciation for the job that you are doing. In conclusion, I learned a great deal from you. Some of the lessons you began to teach me are just now making sense, and for that I thank you.

If this person had realized these things while still working for that man, the relationship could have been much different. A good deal of conflict could have been avoided. Our employers are placed in our lives not always because they are the best, but because God can use them as instruments to work off the rough edges of our lives and to conform us to the image of Jesus. Work at your relationship with your employer. Cultivate an attitude of support and submission to authority. That can alleviate the possibility of conflict in one of the most important relationships of your life.

Then there's the possibility of conflict with fellow employees. Sometimes you will have co-workers who share with you a common commitment to the person of Jesus Christ, but you begin to observe things in their lives that are contradictory to that message. They do things you wouldn't do, say things you wouldn't say, or react in ways that are offensive to you. Not everyone who confesses Christ as Savior is a mature, discipled believer. Remember, children act in childish ways.

I think this is extremely important. If you are seeking to evangelize unbelievers on the job, what's your role toward those who are believers? It's to edify, encourage, and help them move toward spiritual maturity. In some cases, you can say, "You know, I took a discipleship training class at my church, and it really made a difference in my growth as a Christian. Sometime you might want to get involved in one of those. It would strengthen your commitment to the Lord." Be proactive rather than reactive. Instead of badmouthing them because they don't measure up to your standard of what a Christian ought to be, help them grow in grace. Encourage them. Share what you have learned along the way. Build bridges of respect and mutual support to eliminate the possibility of conflict with your Christian co-workers.

With respect to avoiding conflict with those who are unbelievers, we find some practical advice in 2 Thessalonians 3:

> *In the name of the Lord Jesus Christ, we command you, brothers, to keep away from every brother who is idle and does not live according to the teaching you received from us. For you yourselves know how you ought to follow our example. We were not idle when we were with you, nor did we eat anyone's food without paying for it. On the contrary, we worked night and day, laboring and toiling so that we would not be a burden to any of you. We did this, not because we do not have the right to such help, but in order to make ourselves a model for you to follow. For even when we were with you, we gave you this rule: "If a man will not work, he shall not eat" (vv. 6–10).*

First of all, this passage makes it very clear that a Christian should not be idle. Anytime we labor alongside other people, we should not slough off and do less than our share of the work.

Recall Jesus' conversation with Peter following the Resurrection. After Jesus reconciled himself with Peter and forgave him of his betrayal (John 21:15–19), Peter asked what the Lord would do about John. And Jesus said, in essence, "What is that to you? You must follow me" (v. 22). What a rebuke! And I believe it underscores Paul's counsel to the Thessalonians: When we go to work, each of us is responsible for the task we were hired to do. When we don't bear our responsibility, our co-workers suffer. Either our employer hires more people to do what we don't do, or those who work beside us have to do more than their share to make up for our neglect. Paul says this isn't right. Every Christian must do the part of the job for which he is hired. When we do our job and do it well, we eliminate an important cause of conflict with others in the workplace.

Second, Paul goes on to advise his Christian friends not to associate with the resident busybodies:

We hear that some among you are idle. They are not busy; they are busybodies. Such people we command and urge in the Lord Christ to settle down and earn the bread they eat (2 Thess. 3:11–12).

Do you have busybodies in the place where you work? I hope you're not one of them. Some workplaces are like continuing soap operas; every idle moment leads to a conversation about what's going on in the lives of other employees. This should not be. We don't go to work to socialize. We're not paid to socialize. I think we Christians need to use keen discernment about what we do on company time. If we want to share the plan of salvation with someone in the workplace, we shouldn't do it on company time. Let us never be accused of using the time, for which we are paid to do our employer's business, as time to do God's business. It can cause conflict.

Finally, Paul gives us this plain counsel about working alongside other people: "And as for you, brothers, never tire of doing what is right" (v. 13). This certainly is a practical way to eliminate conflict with our employers and co-workers. Paul enlarges on this advice in Romans 12:18: "If it is possible, as far as it depends on you, live at peace with everyone." Aren't you glad Paul had the insight to say "If it is possible"? He implies that in some situations, as hard as you try, you can't be at peace with your boss or with your fellow employees. It's beyond your control. You can do all the right things, but if you aren't met halfway by your employer or your fellow employees, it just won't work. You may say, "Well, I give up on that one. It was worth a try." But notice what Paul says in the context of Romans 12:

Bless those who persecute you; bless and do not curse. Rejoice with those who rejoice; mourn with those who mourn. Live in harmony with one another. Do not be proud, but be willing to associate with people of low position. Do not be conceited. Do not repay anyone evil for evil. Be careful to do what is right in the eyes of everybody. If it is possible, as far as it depends on you, live at peace with everyone (vv. 14–18).

Your actions are what God holds you accountable for. He doesn't hold you accountable for the boss's response. He doesn't hold you accountable for your fellow worker's response. He only holds you responsible for doing all you can to develop peace.

Do not take revenge, my friends, but leave room for God's wrath, for it is written: "It is mine to avenge; I will repay," says the Lord. On the contrary: "If your enemy is hungry, feed him; if he is thirsty, give him something to drink. In doing this, you will heap burning coals on his head." Do not be overcome by evil, but overcome evil with good (Rom. 12:19–21).

We're back to that "exceptional living" stuff, aren't we? It isn't good enough to go into the workplace and be good and do all the things people normally deem to be right. As Christians, we are called to take it a step higher. In the workplace we are called to be Christ to our employers and fellow employees. We don't curse them when they curse us; when they smack us on the right cheek, we turn to them the left; when they compel us to go with them a mile, we go with them two; if they sue us for the coats on our backs, we give them our cloaks also; and if the balances are in discrepancy, so that the company owes us more than we owe them, we leave it up to God in His time and His way to settle the score. We don't try to do that ourselves.

Does this mean you should let people use you as a doormat? No. There may come a time when you say to your employer, "As much as I respect you for who you are and the position that God has given you over me, I cannot continue to be treated as you're treating me. I think it best that I move on to another place of employment." You can do that in a loving, Christlike manner. But until God leads you to do it, be as Christ to that employer.

The same applies to fellow employees. They may talk behind your back; they may wrongly accuse you of things; they may cause you not to get the promotion you think you deserve. The natural response is to say, "I'll get even with them." But the Spirit of God in you says, "No, love them. Don't overcome evil with evil, but overcome evil with good."

A man discovered that one of his fellow employees was making life difficult for him. The man was saying ugly, negative things behind his back. One day, the Christian could take it no longer. Feeling deeply offended by what his co-worker was saying, he went home that night to plot his revenge. As he prayed, God simply reminded him, "Do not overcome evil with evil, but overcome evil with good."

"But, Lord," the man protested, "he doesn't deserve good. Haven't You noticed what he's done to me? Haven't You noticed what I've had to suffer because of him? I have my rights!"

God reminded him that Christ surrendered those rights a long time ago, and now he had to surrender his rights in order to be Christlike in his workplace. That young man couldn't sleep until he got on his knees and said, "All right, Lord, tomorrow morning I will find a way to overcome evil with good."

Suddenly, he had an idea. He and his wife had been out to dinner a few weeks earlier at a new restaurant in town. It was one of the most fabulous places they had ever found. The food was good; the atmosphere was great; there was even live entertainment that they enjoyed. He remembered that, as he was checking out, somebody was buying a gift certificate. He said, "Lord, tomorrow morning I'll buy this fellow a gift certificate to that restaurant."

On his way to work, he found the manager was working early in the restaurant. He bought the gift certificate and took it to work with him. He said to his fellow employee who had done him wrong, "I just want to show my appreciation for you. I know the last few weeks have been rough on you. I don't know what you're going through, but I want you to know that I love you in Christ and I care. My wife and I enjoyed this restaurant recently and we think you would, too. I just want you to take your wife and try it. You'll need to do it within the next two weeks, because there's an expiration date on the coupon. If you don't do it within the next two weeks, it's worthless."

What the young man didn't know was that his co-worker's marriage was breaking up. Their teenage son had been arrested and thrown into jail the week before for delinquent behavior. So the man went home and said to his wife, "This character at work gave me this gift certificate to a restaurant. It's got our names on it. If we don't use it in the next two weeks, it's wasted. So let's go to dinner tonight."

The couple went to the new restaurant that night. They enjoyed a meal and, for the first time in weeks, they talked to each other. They had been too busy to do that before. So they talked. Later that evening, as they were lying in bed about to go to sleep, the husband said, "You know, we've placed a very valuable relationship in jeopardy—ours. After tonight, I think it's worth saving. We really ought to recommit to working on it."

A couple days passed. The son came by the house and said, "Dad, I need to talk to you."

His father said, "I need to talk to you. You embarrass me by your behavior. You embarrassed me when your name appeared in the newspaper because you'd been arrested."

The boy said, "Yeah, Dad, and I think I know why I did what I did. It got your attention. Negative attention is better than no attention at all."

Before his father could respond, the boy continued, "I heard what you did with Mother the other night. You took her out to dinner. That's the first decent thing you've done for her in years. She told me she had a great time."

The father broke down in tears. He said, "Son, I need your forgiveness. I owe you an apology."

Healing began in that family, all because an employee, abused by another to the extent that he was ready to "settle the score," obeyed the promptings of the Holy Spirit instead.

It defies human thinking to believe that you can overcome evil with good. The human response is to say, "Hit it head-on, eye for eye, tooth for tooth. I have my rights!" But Jesus says, "Even when they betray you, stoop down and wash their feet. When they curse and deny that they ever knew you, pray for their forgiveness. When they drive the nails into your hands and they press the crown of thorns into your brow, say, 'Father, don't lay this sin against their charge.' See them through God's eyes."

We can meet conflict in the workplace by engaging redemptively with other people. We can influence them by a life that is exceptional. We can go beyond being good to being Christlike.

7

My Attitude Toward My Witness

As Jesus was walking by Lake Galilee, he saw two brothers, Simon (called Peter) and his brother Andrew. They were throwing a net into the lake because they were fishermen. Jesus said, "Come follow me, and I will make you fish for people." So Simon and Andrew immediately left their nets and followed him (Matt. 4:18–20, New Century Version).

"I'm going fishing." Those were the words of Peter to the disciples when the resurrected Lord had not appeared. Six decided to go with him—back to the humdrum of the daily routine they had known before (John 21:3). They had not yet experienced the resurrected Christ and probably had forgotten that prophetic word He had spoken: "I will make you fish for people." But not many days later, they experienced an event that we call Pentecost (Acts 2). Endued with the power of the resurrected Christ and anointed with the power of the Holy Spirit, they went out to "turn the world upside down" (see Acts 17:6), to be witnesses of God's redeeming love to anyone anywhere who would listen to the message of Christ's love.

We who follow Christ are called to go fishing in His name, too, and we have no better place to "fish for people" than in the workplace. There, apart from our homes, we spend the bulk of our time. There, as in no other place, the message of Christ's love is needed so desperately. We have seen that most of the task of witnessing is accomplished through our transformed attitudes—our attitude toward our employer, our fellow employees, and our work. We consider our work to be a calling, not a job. Our attitude toward conflict in the workplace is to act as God's peacemakers, instruments of righteousness and reconciliation, even among those who do not profess Christ's name.

A woman who works in our church office recently shared with me concerning the difference between working in a church office and in the business world. She related how her daughter had called her on the phone at her job one day needing a verse of Scripture to reinforce a belief she was sharing with a nonbeliever. The woman recalled the reference, much to her daughter's delight, but was somewhat shocked when later she was called on the carpet by her superior for having done so. A co-worker had reported her for spending work time on the phone talking religion. It seems the employee who filed the report was one who had been passed over for the promotion she had recently received. It was only the first of several manifestations of jealousy the woman was called on to endure. Loving her jealous co-worker was a challenge but her only option as a believer.

Challenges to witness abound.

But how specifically do we go "fishing for people"? How do we actually behave as the persons God wants us to be in the places where He's put us to serve? Here are three observations:

First of all, *we win other people to Christ as we serve them through our love.* One day an attorney came and asked Jesus a question, "What is the greatest of all the commandments?" Jesus said to him, "Thou shalt love the Lord thy God with all thy heart, mind, body and strength." Jesus continued, "And the second is like unto the first. Thou shalt love thy neighbor as thyself." Jesus suggested that the first and the second commandments of love are inseparable. You can't have one without having the other. Don't ever lose sight of the responsibility to love your neighbor (see Matt. 22:34–40; Mark 12:28–34).

Luke 10 tells us that the attorney would not be undone. He said to Jesus in response, "Who then is my neighbor?" (v. 29).

Many of us think we know who our neighbor is, but we don't see the situation as Jesus does. In Jesus' language, our neighbor is not simply the person who lives next door, across the street, or behind us. Our neighbor is anyone in need—anyone who needs us to draw close to them and be their companions in the time of their pain. Most of us really don't want to get involved with people and their problems. It's very time-consuming. Generally, their demands come at terribly inconvenient times. Such involvement can be extremely costly. That's what we think, isn't it? We begin to see people as interruptions, not as opportunities. But if we're really to win them to Christ, we must be there for them, no matter what the cost.

In Indiana, we only know our neighbors about nine or ten months out of the year. We close ourselves up in our homes during winter, and it isn't until spring that we renew these relationships and begin to talk to the neighbors next door. I saw that so vividly in a neighborhood where we once lived. A young couple lived across the street, and I developed a friendship with them. Vicki and I prayed for them because they wanted a child that they could not have. Finally, the day came when they crossed the street to make the announcement, "Guess what? We're pregnant. God's giving us a child!"

A little boy was born to that couple. He grew to become the apple of his father's eye. But one spring day I was outside, perhaps mowing our lawn for the first time that season, when the young father came across the street and said, "You know, I needed you a few months ago, in the middle of winter."

"Why didn't you call me?" I asked.

He said, "Well, you know, I hadn't seen you for a few weeks. But we got through it OK."

"Got through what?"

"O well, our son's been awful sick, almost died. We found out that he's a brittle diabetic. Things got so bad that I just thought if I'd have come across the street, you'd pray with me or something. I just wish you'd have been there for me."

I asked if I'd done anything to communicate that I wasn't available. "It wasn't that," he said. "It just wasn't convenient. But things are different now. Things are better."

That conversation drove home to me how there are times when people are more open to spiritual things. When crises leave them more perplexed and bewildered, not knowing which way to turn, they just want to know that we will be there for them—to cry with them and let them know that we really care. Such crises often open the door to building a relationship that allows us ultimately to share the love of Christ that we've experienced in our own hearts. I suggest to you that one of the ways in which we "fish for people" is to be good neighbors. Neighbors can be across the street, next door, in the workplace, or stranded on the highway. They're people to whom we can draw near and show the love of Christ.

Second, *we win other people to Christ when we influence them by our lifestyle.* We're never going to introduce anyone to Christ simply by being good. The scribes and the Pharisees of Jesus' day were good people, but Jesus said in the Sermon on the Mount that "except your righteousness exceeds that of the Pharisees," you're not worthy to be a part of the kingdom (Matt. 5:20). We need to learn how to turn the other cheek, walk the second mile, give our coat as well as the cloak, overcome evil with good, seek no revenge or retaliation, love the unlovely, and repay evil with good, even when it's not deserved. Until we can lift our commitment to Christ to that level—above and beyond the good, moral lifestyle of others—it will be difficult to get people to listen to us when we say that Christ has transformed our lives.

I challenge you to examine your lifestyle. One of the qualifications of elders at our church is that they live a "separated lifestyle." Paul said to the Corinthians, "Wherefore come out from among them and be ye separate, saith the Lord." (2 Cor. 6:17). This does not mean we must come out of the world, but we must keep the world out of us. We must live a life that is so distinctively different by our habits and actions that nothing we do will ever be a stumbling block to someone else.

The most troubling social issue for Christians of Paul's day was eating meat that was offered unto idols. Paul said he saw nothing wrong with eating that meat, but some of his Christian brothers did. If other Christians believed it was wrong, and if Paul's eating meat offered to idols would cause my brother to stumble, Paul said, he would not eat another bite of meat as long as he lived. That would be a small price to pay for the credibility of Paul's witness in the lives of those people.

Social drinking is a similar issue among Christians today. Our society takes for granted many other activities, such as gambling, and viewing "soft" pornography on television. I believe that avoiding these things is a prerequisite to being an effective witness in the workplace. It indicates a level of spiritual maturity that God expects of every Christian.

Third, *we win others to Christ through what we say about Him.* There comes a time when we've got to talk explicitly about Jesus. In Acts 3, Peter and John are going to the house of prayer when they see a lame man carried to the gate of the temple to beg. They say, "In the name of Jesus Christ of Nazareth, rise up and walk." (v. 6). He is healed and he walks, a new person. Peter and John are thrown into prison for this miracle of healing. They're brought before the Tribunal to explain the cause of the disturbance that they have created, and they simply answer, "We cannot but help speaking about what the things which we have seen and heard" (Acts 4:20). What a defense!

They didn't say, "We have been to seminary, and we took Theology 101. We've got seminary degrees, so we know how to expound the theology of salvation." No, they said, "We want to tell you about the things that we've seen, heard, and experienced in our own lives." They did something that every one of us is capable of doing equally as well. As they shared their stories, God gave power to their witness.

I preached one evening in the city of Portland, Oregon. The people of the church took me out to eat after the service and in the group was a woman whom I had not met. I introduced myself and asked, "What do you do?"

She said, "I'm the secretary of Senator Mark Hatfield."

"Excuse me, I have a question," I said. "Is he for real? He claims to know Christ as his Savior. He gives the appearance of being sincere in his Christian witness. But you work with him, so give me the real scoop."

She said, "Dr. Lake, if ever there was a godly man who lives what he professes, it's him. I see it every day. He's one of the most Christlike men that I've ever met."

That's power. When I returned home from that encounter, I picked up a magazine that included an article by Senator Hatfield in which he said that, apart from the day he found Christ as his Savior, the most exciting day of his life was when he made Jesus Lord of his life. That day he asked the Lord to give him the freedom to speak His name as freely as he would speak the name of his own wife, his children, or his very best friend. Shortly thereafter, he had a conversation with a man who was virtually an agnostic. Senator Hatfield found Jesus coming into the conversation as frequently as any other name that he mentioned. It was just natural for him to talk about his best friend, Jesus. From that day, he has found liberty to speak Jesus' name wherever he goes.

All of us need that liberty to bring Jesus into our conversations, to exalt Him in the midst of other people, to speak about Him without embarrassment. Ultimately, someone's going to say, "I don't know how to follow Jesus." Then we'll need to tell them how.

One of our men recently said to me, "Charles, I shared Christ this week with a 71-year-old man. As I began to share with him, I saw perplexity on his face, as though I was telling him something he never had heard before. I finally just stopped and said, 'Haven't you ever heard this before?' The man said, "No. No one in all my years has ever shared with me how I could find Christ.'"

My layman said, "I shared the Four Spiritual Laws with him. When I came to the end, he said, 'Can I make that commitment of my life to Christ right now?'" They prayed together and the elderly man received Christ into his life.

It doesn't matter whether you share the "Roman Road " or the "Four Spiritual Laws" or just tell someone how you became a Christian. You should know some way to share Christ with another person. Share the gospel with the lost, and leave the results to the Lord. He'll take over from there. That's the way to "go fishing for people."

Evangelism is truly like fishing in many ways, so let me pass along these six tips for Christian anglers:

(1). **Courageously risk sharing the bait.** No one likes rejection. It's painful. But you'll never catch a fish till you throw the bait into the water. You need to be forthright in telling people about Jesus Christ.

(2). **Discern the right moment to cast the line.** There are times of greater opportunity to reach someone for Christ. Let the Holy Spirit prepare the way for you. Obey the promptings the Spirit gives.

(3). **Select the right bait for the fish.** We forget that Jesus didn't tell everyone that was an unbeliever, : "Ye must be born again." In fact, the gospels indicate there was only one man to whom He ever said that. To a rich young ruler, Jesus said, "Go sell everything you have and give to the poor." (Mark 10:21). To a farmer, He talked about tearing down his barns and building greater ones. To another farmer, He talked about a sower who went out and sowed seeds. Jesus used many different motifs to share the gospel. With some creativity, we can share Christ with a great variety of people to whom the Lord opens the door. We need to fit the bait to the fish.

(4). **Wait patiently for the fish to take the bait.**

(5). **Persevere, never getting discouraged.** If it takes your lifetime or the lifetime of someone you are trying to bring to Christ, remember that the alternative is much worse. Without Christ, a person will be lost eternally without hope of redemption. So don't give up until all opportunity is past. And in the midst of it all, remember to. . .

(6). **Keep yourself out of sight.** Don't ask people to become like you. Ask them to become like Jesus. Keeping Him in the forefront, share your love with those who need to know the Lord.

Representing Christ in the workplace in the twenty-first century provides some unique and unusual challenges. There are risks. You could even lose your job. There are varying degress of freedom in different venues. Although company policies may prohibit the verbal expression of your faith in some offices, few if any can prohibit you from living a godly lifestyle and demonstrating Christlike attitudes toward all aspects of your work. Even a silent witness has power.

I'm going fishing. I hope you'll go with me. It's immensely rewarding, and it's the very purpose for which God sends us into the world.